Barbara Pierce Bush

Barbara Pierce Bush

****

1925–

BY JUDITH E. GREENBERG

CHILDREN'S PRESS®
A Division of Grolier Publishing
New York   London   Hong Kong   Sydney
Danbury, Connecticut

To Helen Carey McKeever, a mentor, partner, and friend

Consultant: LINDA CORNWELL
                   Learning Resource Consultant
                   Indiana Department of Education

Project Editor: DOWNING PUBLISHING SERVICES
Page Layout: CAROLE DESNOES
Photo Researcher: JAN IZZO

Visit Children's Press on the Internet at:
http://publishing.grolier.com

Library of Congress Cataloging-in-Publication Data
Greenberg, Judith E.
    Barbara Pierce Bush, 1925– / by Judith E. Greenberg
       p. cm. — (Encyclopedia of first ladies)
    Includes bibliographical references and index.
    Summary: A biography of the down-to-earth wife of the forty-first president of the
United States, describing her childhood, marriage, family life, political activities, and
volunteer work for such causes as literacy and AIDS.
    ISBN 0-516-20475-0
    1. Bush, Barbara, 1925– —Juvenile literature. 2. Presidents' spouses—United States—
Biography—Juvenile literature. [1. Bush, Barbara, 1925– . 2. First ladies. 3. Women—
Biography] I. Title II. Series.
E883.B87G74 1999
973.929′092—dc21   98–45255
[B]   CIP
                                                             AC

Table of Contents

Barbara Pierce Bush

CHAPTER ONE

Barbara Pierce Bush, the Early Years

✶ ✶ ✶ ✶ ✶ ✶ ✶ ✶ ✶ ✶ ✶ ✶ ✶ ✶ ✶

As the nation's First Lady, Barbara Bush was lovingly referred to by several different names. To most Americans, she was the "grandmotherly" First Lady. The "silver fox" was a name her children often called her as she was foxy (clever) about raising them. The Secret Service code name for her was "Tranquility" because on the surface she always appeared calm. But none of these nicknames tells the whole story of the woman who became the First Lady in 1989.

On June 8, 1925, Barbara Pierce was born into the family of Pauline and Marvin Pierce. She had an older sister, Martha, and an older brother James. She and

✶ ✶ ✶ ✶ ✶ ✶ ✶ ✶ ✶ ✶ ✶ ✶ ✶ ✶ ✶

Portrait of America, 1925: Roaring Along

★ ★

Barbara Pierce was born at the height and heart of the "Roaring Twenties," one of the most energetic decades in American history. It began with women winning the right to vote in 1920; it ended with the stock-market crash of 1929 and the start of the Great Depression. Halfway between, in 1925, however, the Jazz Age was in full swing.

Everything about the year—the decade, in fact—roared with life. The cities bustled with the high culture of music, art, and theater, and with the low life of organized crime. The economy boomed. American wages increased, so people worked fewer hours and had more leisure time. Consumers hankered after the new goods on the market: autos, radios, and other luxuries grew more affordable. Hardworking Americans, it seemed, were ready to have some fun.

America's youth led the charge. Men donned raccoon coats and baggy suits. Young women, called "flappers," "bobbed" their hair, shortened their skirts, and rolled down their stockings. They shocked their elders with smoking and "jiggly dancing." The younger generation thrived on fads such as dance marathons and roller-skating, and they spoke a new slang. Adults cringed over words such as "baloney" (nonsense), "swell" (marvelous), "crush" (a liking for someone), and "goofy" (silly).

A flowering of literature and music marked the best of the year. Published in 1925, F. Scott Fitzgerald's masterpiece *The Great Gatsby* portrayed the shallow side of life in the Jazz Age. The rhythms of jazz, the exciting new music made popular by artists such as Louis Armstrong and Bessie Smith, rose out of Harlem. From that New York neighborhood, black writers and musicians of the 1920s made a lasting mark on American culture.

Ordinary people hungered for entertainment, and they flocked to extravagant movie palaces to swoon over their favorite silent film stars, especially the sleek sheik Rudolph Valentino. Sports heroes rivaled movie stars in popularity, with

Babe Ruth, Red Grange, and Jack Dempsey topping the list. Attendance at sporting events soared.

At the same time, the nationwide law against the sale of liquor that had begun in 1919 was having some unintended side effects. Promoters of Prohibition had hoped that without alcohol, the country would be a better place. Instead, people spent a lot of time and money to obtain liquor illegally. Thousands of secret nightclubs called speakeasies sold drinks illegally to elegantly dressed patrons who knew the password. Many people made their own alcohol in bathtubs and basements. Others smuggled it in from Canada. Worst of all, organized crime built its powerful and deadly empire on bootlegging, or manufacturing and selling liquor illegally.

In 1925, from Harlem to Hollywood, life for Americans around the 48 states roared along at a furious pace.

Martha were close, but her brother often teased and frightened her. Barbara really enjoyed being the baby of the family until 1930 when a second brother, Scott, was born. Scott Pierce was a sickly baby and Mrs. Pierce spent a great deal of time with him. That made Barbara feel left out, and she turned to her father for the attention and love she needed.

Barbara's father was an athlete and a scholar who had a good sense of humor and enjoyed talking with his

Barbara's mother, Pauline Pierce, spent much of her time caring for her ailing son Scott.

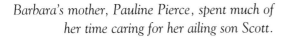

11

Franklin Pierce (1804–1869)

✯ ✯

A handsome and well-spoken lawyer, Franklin Pierce suffered through much personal and presidential turmoil in his life. Born and raised in New Hampshire, he was a bright student and graduated from Bowdoin College in 1824. He married Jane Appleton in 1834, though she never approved of the political career for which he seemed headed. After his undistinguished service in the Mexican-American War during the 1840s, he was nominated as the Democratic candidate for president in 1852. "We Polked you in '44, we'll Pierce you in '52," chanted Democrats, referring to the party's last successful candidate, James Polk. Indeed, Pierce, went on to win the presidency. Just before he took office, however, his young son Ben was killed in a train accident. The tragedy plunged Jane Pierce into a great sadness from which she never recovered and cast a shadow over Franklin's single term in office. Though charming and polished, "Handsome Frank" proved to be an ineffective leader, unable to change the course of America as it headed toward Civil War.

young daughter. He was a successful businessman, and the family lived a secure and comfortable life. Barbara's family was related to the fourteenth president of the United States, Franklin Pierce. This, along with their wealth and intelligence, gave them status in the community of Rye, New York, a suburb of New York City. Barbara's family lived in a handsome brick house. She remembers the gardens and a pond making it the perfect

The Pierce family home in Rye, New York

New York, U.S.A.

✧ ✧

Barbara Pierce was born in New York, the Empire State, in 1925. New York stretches from the Atlantic Ocean west to the Great Lakes and north to Canada. The great metropolis of New York City occupies its southernmost corner, while lovely farms and forestlands cover most of its 47,000 square miles (121,730 square kilometers). It became the eleventh state in 1788, and its capital was established at Albany in 1797. Barbara's hometown, the little waterfront community of Rye, was founded in 1660. It is the oldest permanent settlement in Westchester County. It grew as an overnight stop along the old Post Road to Boston in the 1770s and later became a center of oystering. By 1925, Rye was a popular suburb of New York City. Though only 25 miles (40 km) north, Rye was a world away from the bustle of New York City in the roaring 1920s.

Barbara's father, Marvin Pierce, was a descendant of President Franklin Pierce.

Barbara at the age of six

place to grow up. There was even a tree house that her father built for the boys. Barbara managed to climb it and was called a tomboy for doing so!

In her memoirs, Mrs. Bush talks about going to the movies on Saturday to watch children's adventure films. She also says that some of her happiest times were spent with her father as he walked with her to the school bus on the way to his train to New York City.

Her father was Barbara's favorite parent, but he was often busy as an executive in New York. In 1946, he became president of the McCall Publishing Company. Barbara's mother was a traditional mother of the 1920s and 1930s. She stayed home to take care of her children and often did community volunteer work. She was a very attractive woman who liked

What Evil?

✶ ✶

When Barbara was a child in the days before television, families crowded around their radios to enjoy a variety of suspense-filled dramas. For nearly 25 years, the mysterious crime-fighting Shadow thrilled radio audiences both young and old. He first appeared as a narrator for *Detective Story Hour* in 1930, chilling listeners with tales of crime and evildoings. "What evil lurks in the hearts of men?" the Shadow asked in his haunting voice, raising goosebumps from coast to coast. In 1937, the Shadow himself became a player in each drama, assuming various identities to fight crime with his uncanny ability to "cloud men's minds" by hypnosis. So popular was the Shadow that he also starred in his own series of 325 published stories, comic strips, books, and even films. Although his radio days ended in 1954, the Shadow lives on as one of America's best-loved "pulp" heroes, appearing most recently in a 1994 movie.

beautiful surroundings and ran up huge bills. She also liked to work in her garden.

Barbara's father loved all sports and encouraged Barbara's love of bike riding and sports in general. She also took tennis, swimming, and dancing lessons. As a child, she greatly enjoyed reading stories—especially those about dogs—and playing dress-up and make-believe. The whole family enjoyed reading, and the house was filled with books, magazines, and encyclopedias. In one bookcase was a radio. Barbara remembers the family listening to a popular, scary radio program called *The Shadow*.

The Pierces, members of a wealthy community, had household help. Some of Barbara's favorite childhood memories are of the delicious food they all ate as they sat around the table with mother at one end and father at the other. She says her mother used to tell Martha to eat everything but warned Barbara not to!

When Barbara was a child, her father often traveled with her from New York to Dayton, Ohio, on a sleeper train like this one.

When Barbara was only about five or six years old, her father took her on business trips to Dayton, Ohio. They traveled on a sleeper train. This was a typical way to travel then, and such trains had compartments with very narrow beds so travelers could sleep as the train went on its way. These trips were quite an adventure for a young girl. Barbara remembers that a female attendant on the train would get her ready for bed. The next day, her grandparents would meet the train and take her to their home while her father went to business meetings.

Mrs. Pierce tried to make her children better behaved and was the parent who did the scolding in their family. Spanking a disorderly or rude child was quite acceptable in those days. It seems that brother Jimmy got most of the spankings! The younger brother, Scott, spent much of his childhood having surgery to correct a problem in his arm. Mrs. Pierce went back and forth to the hospital in New York to help take care of him. The brother and sisters agreed that Scott was the kindest of the four children.

As a young girl, Barbara was popular and fun-loving and idolized her beautiful, slender, older sister. Barbara had five close girlfriends in her neighborhood. They enjoyed playing with paper dolls and listening to the radio. Barbara and her friends also enjoyed

Lindbergh Baby Kidnapped!

☆ ☆

Terror struck the hearts of American families on March 1, 1932. That night, a mysterious stranger crept into the quiet New Jersey home of Anne and Charles Lindbergh and kidnapped Charles Jr., their 20-month-old son. The baby's father, "Lucky Lindy," was an American hero who had flown the first nonstop flight from New York to Paris in 1927. That the peaceful security of his home could be violated sent shock waves through Americans everywhere. Though the Lindberghs paid a $50,000 ransom, the child was found murdered six weeks later. It took two years for police to apprehend Bruno Hauptmann, an illegal German immigrant, and charge him with the crime. The public followed the news about Hauptmann's trial and execution hungrily. Publicity surrounding the "Crime of the Century" rose to a fever pitch. From his jail cell, gangster Al Capone offered a $10,000 reward for information about the crime. The events even became the subject of a comic strip. To escape the media circus, the grieving family sought solitude on an island in France. As a result of the tragedy, Congress enacted the Lindbergh Law to make kidnapping a federal crime under the jurisdiction of the FBI.

spotting celebrities. One of their favorites was Amelia Earhart. One of the few sad memories of Barbara's childhood was when the Charles Lindbergh baby was kidnapped. It frightened adults as well as children that the son of an American hero could be murdered.

It was expected that young people growing up in Rye would attend dance classes on Fridays. So twelve-year-old Barbara dressed up in her silk dress and learned the dance step for that week. Fearing that she might not be asked to dance because of her height—5 feet 8 inches (173 centimeters)—she often hid in the bathroom or volunteered to dance the boy's part if there were not enough males.

Barbara had reddish-brown hair

Amelia Earhart (1897–1937)

No wonder Amelia was one of Barbara's favorite celebrities. She must have seemed every bit the modern woman: rugged, adventurous, independent, and attractive. Famous as a pioneer woman aviator, she had learned to fly despite her family's fearful protests. In 1928, joining a male pilot and navigator, she was the first woman to fly across the Atlantic Ocean. Four years later, she became the first woman to cross the Atlantic solo. Although she married in 1931, she kept her maiden name, which was unusual in those days. She and her husband settled in Barbara's hometown, although Amelia was always on the go setting aviation records for altitude and speed. To publicize the safety of air travel, she once flew First Lady Eleanor Roosevelt to Baltimore, both women wearing evening clothes. She made the first solo flight from Hawaii to the mainland in 1935. Her last challenge came in a round-the-world flight. Bound out of New Guinea near the end of the journey, Amelia's plane was lost over the Pacific Ocean. Although rumors abound as to her fate, no sure evidence of Amelia, her navigator, or her airplane has ever been found.

As a child, Barbara attended Milton School.

When she was older, she went to Rye Country Day School.

and although she worried about her weight, she was very pretty. She attended private schools, first Milton School and then Rye Country Day School. In her tenth-grade class picture, Barbara looks like a very attractive, poised young lady of her time.

For her junior year of high school, Barbara's mother decided to send her to Ashley Hall. This was a preparatory, or finishing, school for girls in Charleston, South Carolina, which Barbara's older sister had also attended. Such schools were popular then and allowed girls time to mature and also learn music, languages, arts,

and sports as well as the regular school subjects. It was a happy time for Barbara as she enjoyed her new friends. She also became active in drama and continued her swimming.

Barbara's time at school was a time for growing up and that even included learning to make speeches—something she hated to do—but it certainly would help her later on in her life when she made speeches on the campaign trail. Unlike teenagers today, teens of Barbara's time did not do very much driving. The Great Depression, a worldwide business slump, was just ending. Many people did not have a car. Those who did could hardly afford

Barbara's Rye Country Day School tenth-grade class picture

When Barbara was a junior in high school, her mother sent her to Ashley Hall, a Charleston, South Carolina, finishing school.

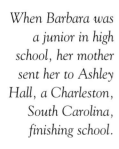

20

Barbara (left) with her sister Martha (holding Barbara's niece), her brother James, her father Marvin, and her brother Scott (holding the family dog)

the gas for it. Riding bikes with a group of girls and boys was more the style in which teens spent a Saturday afternoon. Dating was usually done in groups, and no one got very serious because they were only sixteen. That was soon to change for Barbara Pierce.

It was at a Christmas dance in 1941 that Barbara Pierce met George Bush for the first time. Although George Bush's family lived in Greenwich, Connecticut, not far from Barbara's home, the two had never met. Their parents even belonged to the same country clubs. However, George, nicknamed Poppy, and Barbara did not meet until 1941. She was a high school junior, and he was a senior at Phillips Academy in Andover, Massachusetts. Their schools were many miles apart.

Barbara Bush recalled in her memoirs the night she first met the man she would love for the rest of her life. She was having a wonderful time dancing and seeing friends she hadn't seen during the school year when a friend told her he wanted her to meet a young man named Poppy Bush. They were introduced and spent about fifteen minutes dancing and talking with each other. When Barbara went home that night, she told her mother she had met the "nicest, cutest boy."

The next night, Poppy showed up at another dance Barbara was attending. Later, he went to a game at her brother's school and met the Pierce family. After vacation, both Poppy and Barbara went back to their own schools and wrote to each other as often as possible. By spring break, they longed to see each other, but their vacations overlapped on only one day. They went to a movie, and he invited her to his senior class dance. Barbara had a marvelous time at the dance and decided that George "Poppy" Bush was the most wonderful boy in the world!

The United States had entered World War II in December 1941. George Bush joined the navy on June 12, 1942, just after his graduation from Phillips Academy. He was only eighteen years old. George left for basic training, where new recruits learned about weapons and prepared for the war. In 1942, Barbara appeared in a school production of Shakespeare's *Much Ado About Nothing*. Acting was easier than public speaking for Barbara, and she continued in drama while at school. Within that year, George became a pilot, and Barbara graduated from school and was accepted at Smith College. No one from

George Bush as a young naval pilot

her family came to her graduation because during the war it was thought to be unpatriotic to use gasoline for long trips. Gasoline was needed for the war, and families rarely used their share of gas to go to a graduation.

During Barbara's summer break, George got seventeen days of leave from the navy. His mother invited

22

World War II: Fast Facts

WHAT: The second great global conflict

WHEN: 1939–1945

WHO: The Axis Powers, including Germany, Italy, and Japan, opposed the Allies, including Britain, France, and the USSR. The United States entered the war on the Allied side in 1941 after the bombing by Japan of Pearl Harbor in Hawaii.

WHERE: Fighting raged throughout the Pacific Ocean and in the Atlantic as well as from Scandinavia to North Africa, and deep into the Soviet Union.

WHY: Chancellor Adolf Hitler set out to make Germany the most powerful country in the world, and began by invading his European neighbors. Japan, Italy, and Germany pledged support to one another in 1940. When the United States declared war on Japan after the attack on Pearl Harbor in 1941, Germany and Italy declared war on the United States.

OUTCOME: The war ended in stages. Germany surrendered in May 1945. Japan surrendered after the United States dropped two atomic bombs there in August. More than 400,000 American troops died in battle; about 17 million on both sides perished.

The Bush house in Kennebunkport, Maine

Barbara to come to their home in Maine. This was to be her first trip to Kennebunkport. It was during that vacation that George and Barbara became secretly engaged. Their happiness over their secret was subdued by the fact that George would soon be going overseas to fight in the war. But George's family was very close and everyone worked at keeping the atmosphere happy. They got around by using a horse and buggy instead of a car so they could save on tires and gas!

The days passed quickly until

Barbara (back row, fifth from right) posed for a Smith College class picture.

George had to return to his ship and Barbara to Smith College. They wrote and spoke on the phone whenever possible, but that wasn't often, so Barbara spent her time enjoying the largest school she had ever attended. There were nearly two thousand women at the college. It was the first time Barbara had attended a racially mixed school. She made many friends and even became the captain of the freshman soccer team. Her roommate, Margie Boyce, and Barbara were very close friends. Some people on campus thought it was strange that Barbara never dated, so to avoid gossip, Barbara decided it would be best to announce that she and George were engaged. She chose Christmastime to tell her family, but they already knew! Anyone who saw Barbara and George together had already guessed that they were very much in love and planned to marry. George gave her an engagement ring before he was sent to the Pacific to fight in the war. He was the youngest pilot in the United States Navy, and he flew torpedo bombers.

Barbara's work at school suffered and even she admits that she could

Fashions and Rations

✶ ✶

Americans got used to doing without during World War II. The availability of many necessities such as gasoline, rubber, meat, butter, and sugar was strictly "rationed," or limited. These goods were badly needed for the war effort. Families received ration stamps that allowed them to purchase only limited supplies of such items. Rationing even extended to the fashion industry, as Barbara found out when she tried to buy shoes for her wedding. To save material for uniforms, the government issued strict regulations regarding the amount of fabric a clothing maker could use. Blouses could have only one patch pocket, hoods and cuffs were forbidden, and skirts could measure only 72 inches (183 cm) around. High heels became lower and belts were made narrower to save leather. A shortage of metal zippers made wraparound skirts the rage. American designers rose to the fashion challenge, popularizing sleek-skirted suits and unruffled blouses that used a minimum of fabric. They even created women's wear with a military flair: army caps and jackets inspired a variety of patriotic fashion statements.

have worked harder. She often received letters from George, but because of the war, parts of the letters were cut out by the censors, people who made sure that no military secrets appeared in letters. Sometimes, she got several letters at a time, and then a month might go by without a word.

Through their letters and conversations, they decided that Barbara would leave Smith College and they would marry when George came home in the fall of 1944. Barbara planned to return to college when he went back to his ship. Before this could happen, Barbara and George's family received a dreadful scare. A pilot in George's squadron sent a letter saying that George had been shot down in enemy waters and was last seen swimming toward a life raft. For three agonizing days, they waited for further news.

Finally, they got word from the navy that George had been rescued.

The wedding plans continued even though Barbara had a hard time getting all the things she needed because of the war. Even getting shoes was difficult because they were rationed during the war. Finally, after changing the date of the wedding at least twice because George hadn't been able to get on a flight home, they were married

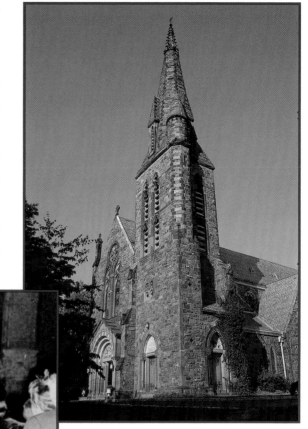

George and Barbara were married in the Rye, New York, Presbyterian Church.

The Pierce-Bush wedding took place on January 6, 1945.

27

The Bushs' first child, George Walker, was born on July 6, 1946.

one another through the difficulties and separations.

George Bush became a war hero and Barbara was very proud of him. After he left the navy, George enrolled in Yale University. Barbara went with him and worked part-time

Famous baseball player George Herman (Babe) Ruth presented the manuscript of his biography to Yale University. George Bush, captain of the Yale baseball team, accepted on behalf of the university.

on January 6, 1945. Barbara was nineteen and George was twenty years old. They honeymooned on an island in Georgia and then spent eight months moving around the country to different air bases where George's squadron was training. The beginning of married life was not easy for Barbara, but she and other service wives helped

While George attended Yale, he and Barbara lived in a two-room apartment for married students in this campus building.

at the school. Their first child, George Walker Bush, was born on July 6, 1946. The happy father graduated two years later with a degree in economics. Not wanting to start out in business by using his family's fortune, George de-cided that the place to go was Texas where there were so many new oppor-tunities for his young family. Once again, Barbara packed up her house-hold and off they went to Odessa, Texas, and then to Midland, Texas.

☆ ☆ ☆ ☆ ☆ ☆ ☆ ☆ ☆ ☆ ☆ ☆ ☆ ☆ ☆ ☆

CHAPTER TWO

Texas, Tragedy, and on to New Places

✮ ✮ ✮ ✮ ✮ ✮ ✮ ✮ ✮ ✮ ✮ ✮ ✮ ✮ ✮

Worln War II had ended. The United States and its allies had defeated the enemy. The country was now a world superpower. The men who had fought so bravely came home expecting to find peacetime jobs. By the time the war was over, however, America had changed. Many women who had taken jobs usually done by the men who had left found they liked working outside the home and earning a paycheck.

It was hard for veterans to find jobs even though employers wanted to hire the returning men. After graduating from Yale, George Bush took some time until he found what he thought he would like to do for

✮ ✮ ✮ ✮ ✮ ✮ ✮ ✮ ✮ ✮ ✮ ✮ ✮ ✮ ✮

a living. He interviewed with many companies and even considered becoming a farmer. Finally, he was offered a job by a classmate and friend of his father. George Bush was about to learn the oil business in Texas.

Barbara and the baby stayed in Maine while George got started in Texas. George began at the bottom, learning everything he could about the oil business. He even painted equipment in the dreadful Texas afternoon heat if that was needed. When George was able to rent a tiny apartment with a bathroom shared with neighbors, he sent for his little family. After a twelve-hour plane trip, Barbara and the baby arrived in Texas. Her first impression was that Texas was incredibly hot and flat! When the wind changed, everyone could smell the oil fields. This was going to be a huge change from New York and Maine! With her usual good spirits and joy at being with her husband, Barbara was happy in Texas, although she did miss her family. She was able to get home for a visit when her brother Jimmy got married. Then tragedy struck.

The Bushes had moved to California for awhile in 1949 so George could work in other kinds of jobs in the oil business. He worked long hours and often seven days a week. One day, he came home early to tell Barbara that her mother and father had been in a terrible car accident and that her mother had died. Because Barbara was pregnant again, she was unable to go to the funeral. This was a very difficult and sad time for her.

Happily, their second child, Pauline Robinson Bush, nicknamed Robin, was born on December 20, 1949, and life began to look better. For Christmas that year, Barbara's father, who had recovered from the accident, gave them a television set! It was big and heavy with a tiny screen. All televisions in those days looked like a big piece of furniture with a only a 7-inch

33

A painting of the Bushes' second child, daughter Robin

(18-cm) screen. But Americans loved television and soon shows such as *Amos and Andy* and *Milton Berle* had the country laughing and watching TV every day. There were only a few channels, and often news and weather were all that was available. Even so, television was starting to change how Americans spent their free time and got their information.

In 1950, the Bushes moved again. They returned to west Texas to a town called Midland. They bought their first house here for $8,000. Barbara loved it. Her days were filled with

The Bushes bought this Midland, Texas, house in 1950.

doing the things she loved most—taking care of her children and husband. In a few years, George and several friends started their own oil company. Another child, John Ellis Bush, nicknamed Jeb, was born in February 1953. The Bushes moved to a larger house, and Barbara and George were very happy with their growing family.

But once again, tragedy struck. This time, their three-year-old daughter Robin became ill with leukemia, a disease of the blood. In those days, there was no cure for this disease and children who had it rarely survived. But Barbara Bush was not about to lose a child without a tremendous fight. Within days, she had friends looking after the two boys. Barbara, George, and Robin flew to a New York City hospital to try to save the child's life. George had to go back to Texas to look after his new business, but Barbara stayed with Robin and worked as hard as any nurse taking care of her little girl.

During this terrible time, Mrs. Bush grew close to many of the other families whose sick children were in the hospital. She never forgot the feelings of helplessness and grief that they all felt.

Robin was a sweet child who took each day as it came and each test or treatment with as much cheer as possible. At times, when Robin felt better, Barbara took her out of the hospital for awhile. Then one day, the treatment that controlled her leukemia began to cause other problems. Robin slipped into a coma and died

Jeb Bush was born in 1953.

The Bushes and their four sons in Midland, Texas, in 1959

ness were so deep that her hair began to turn white.

Barbara tried to deal with her inner pain by spending time with her two boys and doing volunteer work. Then she gave birth to another son, Neil Mallon. In 1956, a son named Marvin joined the growing family. Again, the family moved to a larger house and life became more settled. A dog named Nicky became the family pet, and happy summers were often spent in Maine.

Three years later, George's oil company split up and he moved the family to Houston, Texas. The Bushes built a new house and had another child on August 18, 1959, a girl they named Dorothy Walker Bush, nicknamed Doro. Life for Barbara Bush was steadily getting back to normal. The

the next day. Her death hit Barbara Bush very hard. She busied herself with trying to ease the pain of her other children by helping them understand what had happened to Robin.

This was one of the most difficult periods of Barbara Bush's life. Eight months of trying to save a dying child took a terrible toll. Her grief and sad-

Dorothy Walker (Doro) Bush was born in 1959.

36

Not Home Alone

✫ ✫

As a mother of the baby boom generation, Barbara Bush was among millions of American women raising young families in the 1950s. The 1950s were years of tremendous prosperity in the United States. Americans had suffered through the depression of the 1930s and World War II in the 1940s. They were now ready for the good life. They bought homes in the suburbs, automobiles, and appliances. And they began to have more children. By the end of the decade, the population had increased by 19 percent. Women who had held jobs during the war returned to homemaking, while men commuted to jobs in the city to support their wives and children. Family togetherness in a spacious suburban home seemed to be everyone's dream.

Despite appearances, however, changes were taking place among America's women. During the 1950s, more women entered college than ever before. Between 1940 and 1960, the number of working wives doubled as families realized that it would take two incomes to be able to afford the good life. Women could not earn as much as men, however, and most still worked as typists, nurses, or teachers. The opportunities for female lawyers and doctors were few. So, even though more women were working outside the home as the 1960s dawned, they began to feel frustrated by their limited opportunities. They began to demonstrate for equal rights. Feminism and women's liberation grew strong. Soon, American women who wanted professional lives would never again be limited to finding happiness in the home alone.

boys started to play Little League baseball and soon Barbara was spending her time at games, helping with homework and Sunday school, going to PTA meetings, and setting rules for the children to follow. Because George worked very long hours, Barbara played games with the children, settled their arguments, and bandaged their sores.

Today, many woman think that staying home and caring for children isn't like having a real job. Barbara learned many skills in those days that not only helped her later but probably would have made her an excellent company president.

Marvin, Neil, and Jeb Bush in Houston

She was very organized, often doing several tasks at once and helping neighbors with theirs as well. She also became accustomed to entertaining the large groups of people George often invited to dinner on the spur of the moment. Barbecues and casual entertaining became, and remain, her style.

The chores of raising children and managing family affairs can be boring and are very routine, but doing them helped Barbara realize that she could

Marvin, Doro, and Neil Bush

The Bush family eating at a picnic table at their Houston home

A 1964 family picture of George and Barbara with their five children

Putting Us in the U.S. Government

✫ ✫ ✫ ✫ ✫ ✫ ✫ ✫ ✫ ✫ ✫ ✫ ✫ ✫ ✫ ✫ ✫ ✫ ✫ ✫

The Congress is the chief lawmaking body in the United States. The men and women who serve in Congress are directly elected by the American people. Their job is to make sure that the concerns of the citizens are heard and acted on by the government. Two "houses" make up the Congress: the Senate and the House of Representatives, where George Bush served for four years. In its concept, the U.S. Congress has been around longer than the office of the president. The First Continental Congress met in Philadelphia in 1774, when America was still a collection of English colonies. This first Congress gave the colonists a way to join their voices against high taxes and mistreatment under British rule. It was America's first effort at unity. The Congress as we know it today was formally established by the U.S. Constitution, which outlines its duties. The House of Representatives, as the electoral college, met in 1789 and chose George Washington as the first president. To make the new government work smoothly, the Founding Fathers purposely established a system of "checks and balances" that would separate the powers of Congress and the president. As a result, neither can accomplish much without the other's cooperation. Today, Congress includes 535 members. One hundred senators, two elected from each state, serve six-year terms. The House of Representatives includes 435 members (called representatives or congressmen and congresswomen). The people in each state elect a number of representatives based on the state's population. They serve two-year terms.

handle things well. She developed confidence and a sense of self-worth.

The Bush family was about to make another move—one that would take them away from Texas and into the life of politics. George Bush was elected to the United States House of Representatives in 1966. He was the first Republican to be elected to represent Houston in Congress.

Barbara packed their belongings and the family moved to Washington,

George and Barbara at a rally during George's 1966 congressional campaign

A victory celebration took place at Bush campaign headquarters on November 11, 1966.

D.C. This was the start of the Bushes' life in public service. George's political career brought Barbara many new friends and new skills. She took a public-speaking course and learned the names of all the politicians and their wives so she could help George by being friendly to those people. Most of the politicians at that time were men. Their wives often met for lunch or worked together on volunteer projects. Barbara enrolled the children in schools and learned to be a congressman's wife. She went to Republican meetings, Congressional Wives meetings, and briefings at the State Department. Almost every weekend, George went back to Houston on political business. Barbara and the children stayed in Washington, D.C. They spent their time going to museums and seeing all the monuments. Doro and her mother even stood outside the front gates of the White House wondering what it would be like to live there!

The late 1960s was a particularly interesting time to be living in the

In 1966, during the Vietnam War, peace demonstrators marched in front of the White House.

This stop-the-draft demonstration took place in front of the Oakland, California, city hall in 1968.

nation's capital. During this period, there was unrest over the Vietnam War and over racial issues. Students at universities all over the country began protesting against the war and unfair housing rules that wouldn't let African Americans live in all neighborhoods, and demanding equal rights for minorities and women. Martin Luther King Jr. was killed on April 4, 1968, and riots and fires burned throughout many cities in the country. Just five blocks from the Bushes' house, parts of the city of Washington, D.C., were set on fire.

During George's congressional term, Barbara began writing a month-

Vietnam War: Fast Facts

WHAT: Conflict over control of the Southeast Asian nation of Vietnam

WHEN: 1957–1975

WHO: The United States, South Vietnam, and various allies opposed the North Vietnamese and the Viet Cong

WHERE: Throughout North Vietnam and South Vietnam, and later into Cambodia and Laos

WHY: In the early 1950s, the French controlled Vietnam. Fearing a Communist takeover of Vietnam and the rest of Southeast Asia, American leaders supported the French. When the French withdrew, the United States sent military advisers to help train the South Vietnamese to oppose the Communist north. America became more and more involved until U.S. troops were actually fighting alongside the South Vietnamese in a war against North Vietnam.

OUTCOME: Direct American military involvement ended with a cease-fire in 1973. In all, 58,000 American soldiers and about 1 million North Vietnamese and South Vietnamese perished. In 1975, the North invaded the South, and the capital of Saigon surrendered. Today a unified Vietnam lives under Communist rule.

Martin Luther King Jr. (1929–1968)

✮ ✮

This brilliant and well-spoken Baptist minister became America's leading advocate for civil rights through nonviolence in the 1960s. Born in Atlanta as Michael Luther King, his preacher father later changed both their names to honor the great Protestant reformer Martin Luther. At age fifteen, Martin entered Morehouse College and by eighteen was ordained in his father's church. He continued his education, earning his Ph.D. from Boston University in 1955. A born leader and inspiring speaker, Dr. King rose to prominence urging his followers to practice "passive resistance," or nonviolence, in their quest for civil rights. In doing so, he gave African Americans a powerful new weapon against hate, discrimination, and prejudice. In his most famous speech, delivered in 1963 in a massive march on Washington, Dr. King described his dream that "one day we will live in a nation where [my children] will not be judged by the color of their skin but by the content of their character." Sadly, even the eloquent Dr. King could not hold back the tide of violence that would erupt in the ongoing struggle for civil rights. He himself fell victim to an assassin's bullet on April 4, 1968.

This photograph of (left to right) Jesse Jackson, Martin Luther King Jr., and Ralph Abernathy on the balcony of the Lorraine Motel in Memphis, Tennessee, was taken the night before King was assassinated as he stood on that very same balcony.

44

ly newspaper column for the Houston, Texas, newspapers. The column, "Washington Scene," gave people in Houston an idea of what life was like in the nation's capital. Many congressional wives were starting to have small careers of their own or at least admitting to having graduated from college and professional schools. Things were changing in Washington and in the country. In 1969, Neil Armstrong walked on the moon. In 1970, America was shocked when four protesting college students were killed at Kent State University in a clash with the National Guard.

After four years in Congress, George Bush was appointed United States Ambassador to the United Nations (UN) in 1971. The UN is an organization of world countries that work together for world peace. Bush served as the permanent U.S. representative to the UN. This job meant another move, this time to New York City, the location of UN Headquarters. To train for this new job, the Bushes traveled to Europe to visit some of the UN agencies and organizations in several world capitals. On their re-

Astronaut Neil Armstrong planted a U.S. flag on the surface of the moon on July 20, 1969.

U.S. Ambassador to the UN George Bush (left) during a UN session

A Vice President Resigns

Many Americans were surprised when presidential candidate Richard Nixon chose Spiro T. Agnew as his running mate in the election of 1968. Little was known about Agnew, governor of Maryland, except that he was extremely conservative. However, at a time when the Vietnam War and civil rights had seriously divided the nation, Spiro Agnew's stands against student antiwar protests, black activism, the press, and liberal thinking had a certain appeal. "Spiro Is My Hero" read bumper stickers on the cars of his conservative supporters. But Agnew turned out to be controversial for more than his politics. In 1973, the Justice Department uncovered evidence that as governor of Maryland, Agnew had accepted money from companies in exchange for work from the state. Evidence suggested that he even took bribes as vice president. He also faced charges of not paying income taxes. As part of a plea bargain, Agnew agreed to resign the vice presidency. He served three months probation and paid a $10,000 fine. President Nixon nominated Gerald Ford to replace him, thus ending an embarrassing vice-presidential episode. Only one other vice president has ever resigned the office. In 1832, John C. Calhoun left the service of President Andrew Jackson to become a senator.

turn to New York, they moved into an apartment, and George began his new job. He met and entertained ambassadors from other nations and attended UN meetings. While they lived in New York, Barbara volunteered at the Memorial Sloan-Kettering Cancer Center. Barbara found it very rewarding to help people feel more comfortable when they were so sick.

After George had spent two years at the UN, newly reelected President Richard Nixon named him chairperson of the Republican National Committee in 1973. George's job was to help Republican causes. Barbara grew very close to First Lady Patricia Nixon.

The United States was about to undergo great changes. The peace movement in the country had grown, and President Nixon finally declared the war in Vietnam to be over. Spiro Agnew resigned as vice president in October after being involved in a bribery scandal. President Nixon appointed House minority leader Gerald Ford to the post.

Then the Watergate scandal shocked the country. During the 1972 presidential election campaign, people working for Republicans broke into Democratic headquarters at the Watergate office complex in Washington, D.C. After many months of covering up the wrongdoing, President Nixon—on the verge of impeachment—resigned on August 9, 1974. Gerald Ford was sworn in as the

Ford Takes Office Today.

After many months of covering up his part in the Watergate scandal and on the verge of impeachment, President Richard M. Nixon resigned.

thirty-eighth president of the United States.

Throughout these events, the Bush children were growing up, graduating from college, and getting married. Life was very full for Barbara Bush. In 1974, Jeb Bush got married. That event was one of the only happy times

George and Barbara enjoyed bicycling through the streets of Beijing during their 1974 trip to China.

for the Bush family during the troubled Watergate years.

In 1974, Ford appointed George Bush chief of the Liaison Office in the People's Republic of China. That huge Asian country was just beginning to open up to outsiders. This time, the Bush children did not go with George and Barbara. Doro, the youngest at fifteen, had already decided to go to boarding school, so only C. Fred, Barbara's dog, accompanied them during their stay in China. Barbara was amazed at the foods they ate while in China and even was happy that they

both lost weight while serving there. They bicycled through the streets of Beijing and traveled throughout the country. Barbara especially enjoyed visiting famous old sites and cities.

At the end of 1975, George was called back to the United States to become head of the Central Intelligence Agency (CIA). At the time, the agency had a very bad reputation with many people in the United States. Among other shady operations, it had spied illegally on thousands of Americans who had opposed the Vietnam War. Much of George's time on the

Barbara watched as George Bush (right) was sworn in as director of the CIA in January 1976.

48

Shadow Warfare

★ ★

Spying has been around since governments began to keep secrets. Times of war, especially, call for undercover missions to thwart the enemy. Until World War II, however, the United States had no formal organization to oversee and coordinate such activity. When President Roosevelt made William "Wild Bill" Donovan the director of the Office of Strategic Services (OSS) in 1941, the country had its first agency for gathering "intelligence," or information concerning the enemy. Donovan had actually carried out a spy mission in 1919 while honeymooning in Siberia, of all places. Throughout the war, the OSS and its "shadow warriors" fought secretly against Nazi Germany and Japan by spying, gathering information, sabotaging enemy projects, and cracking codes. But after World War II, what role would spies and codebreakers play? Fears about the spread of Communism from Russia answered that question. In 1947, President Truman signed into law the National Security Act, creating both the Department of Defense and the Central Intelligence Agency (CIA). In the following years, the CIA kept busy masterminding the overthrow of the leftist regime in Guatemala, planning to topple Castro's Communist dictatorship in Cuba, and undertaking covert (secret) actions around the world. Today, more "spies" than decoders work at desks. At the largest division of the CIA, researchers gather and analyze published data regarding the governments, politics, economies, and other vital information about countries around the world.

new job was spent trying to bring the agency back to the standards on which it had been chartered.

By then, Barbara had moved her family to 17 cities and lived in 29 different homes. She had become so good at moving that she could unpack and have the family settled in a week!

One of the Bush family's biggest moves was yet to come—when George decided to run for president in the 1980 election.

CHAPTER THREE

Changing Times and
a Second Lady

✫ ✫ ✫ ✫ ✫ ✫ ✫ ✫ ✫ ✫ ✫ ✫ ✫ ✫ ✫ ✫

The decades of the 1970s and 1980s were a time of change in America, and George and Barbara Bush were a part of it.

The Education Act of 1972 had been signed by President Nixon. It included a section called Title IX. This act prohibited discrimination against girls and women by any school that received federal funds. One result of this act was that schools had to spend money equally on sports for boys and girls. If there were no girls' team, schools had to let girls try out for the boys' team. Finally, by the 1980s, girls' sports teams were getting a much fairer share of schools' sports money. Girls

✫ ✫ ✫ ✫ ✫ ✫ ✫ ✫ ✫ ✫ ✫ ✫ ✫ ✫ ✫ ✫

were learning that it was okay to try to win and to play hard. They were learning to set goals and achieve them through sports. Many girls received college scholarships because they had become such good players.

The next seven or eight years brought many changes to America and to the lives of American women. Children who had been born just after World War II ended now had college educations and careers. Their own children were being raised to know that women and men are equals and should be given equal opportunities.

More women were also being elected or appointed to important positions of power in the United States and throughout the world. Women were news anchors and judges, doctors and heads of large companies. Margaret Thatcher was the prime minister of Great Britain. When Sandra Day O'Connor was appointed to the United States Supreme Court, Barbara Bush attended the Senate confirmation hearings. O'Connor was the first woman to be appointed to this high court. Barbara herself did not aspire to a career. She was very happy

Margaret Thatcher became prime minister of Great Britain in 1979.

being George's wife and helping him with his career.

In January 1979, George Bush began his campaign for the Republican nomination to the presidency. During his campaign, he was often asked what his wife's project would be should George be elected. Most First Ladies choose a special cause or project to sponsor, and Barbara Bush was expected to do the same. For example, Rosalynn Carter was interested in mental health, Pat Nixon focused on

Sandra Day O'Connor (1930–)

✭ ✭

This fifty-one-year-old Texan was the first woman to rise to the highest judgeship in the land when President Reagan appointed her to the United States Supreme Court in 1981. Established in 1788, the Supreme Court's ultimate job is to decide whether the laws of the land follow the intent of the Constitution. The number of justices changed seven times over its first 100 years, and since 1869 has been set at nine. Each justice is appointed by the president and serves for life. Until Justice O'Connor took her place on the bench, the judges had been largely elder statesmen—"a quiet group of old boys," in the words of one. Sandra O'Connor's experience as a lawyer and an Arizona state senator led her to become the first female majority leader in any state senate. Although a conservative, her main concerns lay with gender discrimination and poor families. She supported the women's Equal Rights Amendment. She went on to serve as a trial judge and on the Arizona Court of Appeals. Her reputation for firmness and compassion and her conservative yet fair approach to the law made her a logical choice when President Reagan sought a woman to appoint to the Supreme Court.

volunteerism, and Lady Bird Johnson was an early environmentalist who wanted to make America look more beautiful. Barbara's project would be literacy. This project was important to her as many Americans had difficulty because they were unable to read or write.

Although George Bush did not win the nomination for president, he was

53

As First Lady, Rosalynn Carter was the honorary chair of the President's Commission on Mental Health.

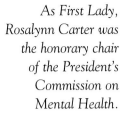

First Lady Patricia Nixon volunteered to help painters at a low-income housing project.

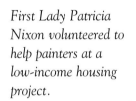

First Lady Claudia (Lady Bird) Johnson helped make America more beautiful.

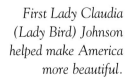

The Bushes and Reagans were running mates during the 1980 presidential campaign.

First Lady Nancy Reagan (left) and Second Lady Barbara Bush in 1981

asked to be Ronald Reagan's running mate as the vice-presidential nominee. With her husband's election, Barbara became the Second Lady of the United States, while Nancy Reagan was First Lady.

Second Ladies have a totally different life than First Ladies. A Second Lady makes many appearances at projects and government functions. She is not on display quite as much as the First Lady, but often substitutes for the First Lady.

The newspapers and television reporters tend to leave the Second Lady alone and concentrate on the First Lady. However, even Second Ladies are expected to be supporters of social

Vice President's Residence

✫ ✫

Everyone knows where the president lives, but what about the vice president? Not until 1974 did the "veep" and his family rate an official home in Washington. Until then, they fended for themselves, living mostly in hotels or rented rooms.

Several early "second men" hung their hats at the Willard Hotel. Established in 1850 just steps from the White House, the Willard was for years Washington's premier hotel. A more-recent version of it stands today. The Lyndon Johnsons were lucky enough to afford their own home, called The Elms, a hilltop French-style chateau secluded by shrubbery. The Nelson Rockefellers actually had five homes in Washington and elsewhere. Finally, in 1974, Congress ordered that the admiral's house on the grounds of the U.S. Naval Observatory (an astronomical observation station) become the vice presidential residence. Built in 1893 for the superintendent of the observatory, the thirty-three-room mansion underwent many needed repairs. In 1977, the Walter Mondales were the first Second Family to move into the official vice president's residence.

causes and to be sensitive to the needs of the American people while their husbands are busy in office.

Barbara and George Bush lived in the vice president's official home, which is on the grounds of the U.S. Naval Observatory in Washington, D.C. It is an old house, built in 1893, and needed a lot of repairs when the Bushes moved in. The Washington

Vice President and Mrs. Bush greeting the Iran hostages in January 1981

Press Secretary James Brady (right front, on the ground) was badly wounded during the March 30, 1981, assassination attempt on President Reagan.

Monument can be seen from a window in the vice president's bedroom.

After the inauguration of President Reagan, one of the Bushes' first official assignments was to greet the freed hostages who had been released from Iran. These people had been held as prisoners for 444 days. They were amazed at the joyous reception they received from the American people.

March 30, 1981, started out as a lovely day for the Second Lady. She attended the Cherry Blossom Festival and a reception for a volunteer group. She lunched with the cabinet wives and attended an afternoon tea with a historical preservation group. When she returned home, Barbara turned the TV on but left the sound off. Suddenly, she saw President Reagan being pushed into a car. People were running around and someone was lying on the ground. There had been an assassination attempt on President Reagan. Fortunately, he was not badly hurt, but Press Secretary James Brady was badly wounded and never fully recovered.

The president of the United States is asked to attend many events such as

In 1982, Barbara and George Bush visited Prime Minister Zenko Suzuki and his wife in Tokyo.

The Bushes also visited Israel during their busy years as the Second Family.

visits from foreign dignitaries, weddings, and funerals. It would be impossible for him to accept all the invitations and run the country too. The vice president and his wife often attend in the president's place. On one occasion, the Bushes entertained the president of France and his wife when they came to the United States to celebrate the festive 200th anniversary of the American Revolution. The French had been very helpful to George Washington's army.

Barbara Bush kept a record of the family's extensive travels during the eight years that George was vice president. They visited all fifty states and

In 1982, Second Lady Barbara Bush (second from left) dedicated the opening of the Betty Ford Center. Also on hand were Vice President George Bush (left), Betty and Gerald Ford, and Dolores and Bob Hope (right).

sixty-five different foreign countries for a total of 1,629 days away from Washington, D.C. One of the highlights was a trip to England to attend the wedding of Prince Charles and Diana Spencer. Barbara estimates that they traveled about 1.3 million miles (2 million km), the equivalent of traveling around the world fifty-four times! When they were in Washington, D.C., Barbara hosted 1,192 events at the vice president's home and went to 1,232 others.

Two of the Bush children married while George was vice president, and Barbara was busy with those happy occasions as well as her Second Lady duties. She put the star on the top of the nation's Christmas tree in 1981 and dedicated the opening of the Betty Ford Center in 1982. Former First Lady Betty Ford wanted to create a place for people to go to when they needed help to quit being dependent on drugs and alcohol. The Bushes also went to the funeral of the leader of the then Soviet Union (now Russia), Leonid Brezhnev.

The year 1982 was also special as it was the year that the Vietnam Veterans Memorial was dedicated in Washington, D.C. This simple monument held tremendous emotional importance for the people who had served in Vietnam and for the loved ones of the nearly 60,000 people who had died there. The names of those who died are engraved on the long, dark, shiny walls. It had taken Americans a long time to recover from the nightmare of this war. Those who fought it never felt appreciated for their service to their country. Some of those who protested the war tried to make the soldiers feel guilty for fighting in the war. This memorial seemed to help heal the wounds.

With her great interest in encouraging people to read and learn, Barbara Bush decided to write a book to raise money. She planned to give the proceeds from the book to Literacy Volunteers of America and Laubach Literacy Action, the two programs she worked with. She was thinking about writing the book from the point of view of her dog, C. Fred. One night while having dinner at the vice president's house with some people from a publishing company, Mr. Bush told a

Barbara Bush's dog, C. Fred

guest to be careful. Apparently, C. Fred was right behind this man, and George didn't want the man to trip on the dog. George called out, "Don't kick that dog. He's writing a book."

What started as a joke, eventually became a book, *C. Fred's Story.* Publication of the book launched Barbara on a literary tour. Wherever she went, she talked about her dog and then put in a plug for literacy. She encouraged people to volunteer to help others learn to read. Sales of the book raised nearly $100,000 for literacy programs.

In the campaign of 1984, Reagan and Bush again ran as the Republican

Barbara Bush at a Boys and Girls Club during a literacy-promotion tour

Walter Mondale (above) was the 1984 Democratic candidate for president. His running mate was Geraldine Ferraro (below).

nominees for president and vice president. The Democrats nominated Walter Mondale for president. His running mate was Geraldine Ferraro. For the first time in the history of the country, a woman was the vice-presidential candidate of a major political party. The newspapers and television reporters wrote a lot about Ferraro, and George Bush did not enjoy the campaign very much. Reagan and Bush won the election, however, and the Bushes continued living in the vice president's house and representing the president abroad.

In 1985, a TWA flight was hi-

Vice President George Bush greeting the TWA hostages in Beirut, Lebanon

George Bush at the Wailing Wall in Jerusalem during a 1986 trip

jacked. The hijackers held the hostages captive on a runway in Beirut, Lebanon. A daring rescue by Canadian troops captured the imagination of people around the world. The Bushes represented the president when the hostages and their families were finally reunited.

The Statue of Liberty was one hundred years old in 1986 and the country celebrated the magic of this symbol of American freedom. Originally a gift from the French people, the Statue of Liberty came to represent freedom to all the people who came to America looking for a new life. The Bushes attended the celebration. A few weeks later, they were in Jerusalem at the Wailing Wall, the remaining holy wall of the Jewish Temple. Like millions of others who visit this special place, Barbara left a note tucked into the wall. She asked for world peace.

When her beloved dog C. Fred died, Barbara was terribly upset. She greatly felt the loss of his company. She and George decided to get another dog. Thus, the famous springer spaniel Millie came to be part of the Bush family.

Making a Stand for Liberty

✦ ✦

"Miss Liberty," "the Mother of Exiles," "Lady with a Torch"—by any name, the Statue of Liberty is among the best-known women the world over. For more than a hundred years, the golden flame she holds boldly aloft has welcomed millions of sea-weary newcomers with the promise of freedom and opportunity. Miss Liberty's own journey to America was none too easy. Given by the French people as a token of friendship, the immense copper statue was created by sculptor Frederic-Auguste Bartholdi. His work began in 1874 with a 4-foot (1.2-m) clay model and ended ten years later with a 225-ton (202-metric-ton), 151-foot (46-m) colossus. Meanwhile, Americans were having a hard time

raising money to build a pedestal on which to mount the statue. To drum up support, Liberty's huge arm and torch were exhibited in New York City and Philadelphia. Still, by the time the statue was completed and ready to ship in 220 crates, no pedestal had been built. Finally, American newspapers launched a campaign to raise the funds, noting the embarrassment of having nowhere to erect the massive lady. Donations poured in and Miss Liberty set sail from France. After being reconstructed atop its 150-foot (46-m) pedestal on a small island in New York Harbor, the statue was dedicated on October 28, 1886.

In 1987, the first family of Russia, Mikhail and Raisa Gorbachev, visited the United States. The Bushes got along well with the Gorbachevs and had many visits with them when George later became president.

After eight years of being the vice president, George Bush decided to run for president. Several Democrats ran for the Democratic nomination, and the field of candidates grew quite large. Massachusetts governor Michael Dukakis finally became the Democrats' choice for presidential candidate.

The Bushes had been partners of

The Bushes greeting the Gorbachevs on their arrival in Washington in 1987

President Ronald Reagan (second from left) endorsed Vice President George Bush as the Republican candidate for president in the 1988 election. With them at the announcement were Nancy Reagan (left) and Barbara Bush.

The Mark of a First Lady

★ ★

Barbara Bush's familiar strands of pearls represented her simple taste and classic style. Her trademark became so popular with the general public that jewelry makers even introduced "First Lady" and "White House" lines of pearl jewelry. In their days, other First Ladies had their own trademarks. Dolley Madison, the lively spouse of fourth president James Madison, favored the fashionable turban, white fabric wrapped around the head and often decorated with plumes. The somber Jane Pierce was known for the black mourning dresses she wore to honor the memory of her son Ben. He had died tragically in a train crash as the family traveled to Washington

for the inauguration of Franklin Pierce as the fourteenth president. For Mrs. Lincoln, none but the finest gowns would do, and extravagance became her trademark. In the 1880s, American women styled their hair like the beautiful young Frances Cleveland. In the mid-twentieth century, pink became the color of choice for everything from clothing to house paint because it was Mrs. Eisenhower's favorite. In the next administration, Jackie Kennedy's trademark pillbox hat represented the height of style.

Dan Quayle (second from left) was George Bush's running mate during the 1988 election campaign.

Michael Dukakis was the Democratic candidate for president in 1988.

the Reagans for eight years, but now they tried to put forth a separate image. Barbara laughed when people compared her to Nancy Reagan. She even joked with reporters that one of her thighs would equal all of Nancy's size-four figure. Barbara refused to dye her white hair or diet or change her style of dress. She was happy as she was, and at age sixty-three thought she would look foolish trying to look younger than her years. Even so, she did admit that her trademark three-strand pearl necklace was worn to cover some of her wrinkles!

Barbara thought her greatest appeal came from looking like every-

one's grandmother. She felt that after all the news articles and television coverage that had been devoted to Nancy Reagan's expensive dresses and costly improvements to the White House, most people would be happy to have a gentle, kindly, older woman in the White House. And she was right! Her warm, no-nonsense approach to life helped win many people to George's campaign. The mail Barbara Bush received showed that people were comfortable with her and trusted her. She did not interfere in George's politics and he appreciated that. In fact, Barbara sometimes disagreed with her husband on issues, but for his

The large Bush family, including all the grandchildren, gathered on the rocks in Kennebunkport, Maine, for a family portrait during an August 1987 summer vacation.

sake, she did not discuss her opinions in public and supported his views.

Barbara Bush thought it would be quite easy to move to the White House and become First Lady. After all, she had been the Second Lady for eight years, and she and George had been involved in government for many years before that. However, all the experience in the world doesn't prepare anyone for the move to the White House.

★　★　★　★　★　★　★　★　★　★　★　★　★　★　★

CHAPTER FOUR

First Lady Barbara Bush

On January 20, 1989, the Reagans greeted the Bushes at the White House and the two couples rode off together for the inauguration ceremonies. United States Supreme Court Justice Sandra Day O'Connor gave the oath of office to Dan Quayle, the vice president, and Chief Justice of the United States Supreme Court William Rehnquist swore in George Bush as president of the United States. Barbara Bush held two Bibles, one that George Washington had used when he took the oath of office and one that had been given to the Bushes as a gift. Holding a special Bible was something she had done each time George Bush

George Bush taking the oath of office as president of the United States

Barbara enjoyed waving to the people who lined the streets during the Inauguration Parade.

had taken an oath of office. Each of their children was given one of the Bibles as a keepsake. After George's inaugural speech, the Bushes escorted former president Ronald Reagan and his wife Nancy to a waiting helicopter and said good-bye.

After lunch, the Inauguration Parade down Pennsylvania Avenue began. It lasted three hours and forty minutes and Barbara Bush had a wonderful time. She waved to friends and even got so excited that she kissed Willard Scott, a popular television personality. He was shocked—and so was Barbara when she realized he was on camera at the time and people all over the world could see that kiss!

To celebrate the swearing-in ceremony, fourteen inaugural balls were held in the city of Washington, D.C. People came from all over the country to attend one of the gala balls held to celebrate the new president. At each of the balls, a Bush relative acted as the host or hostess. Some Hollywood celebrities even joined the festivities. Invitees wore their finest clothes and danced until the early hours of the morning, waiting for the president and

Interesting Inaugurations

☆ ☆

George Bush's inauguration marked two hundred years of American presidents—and of inaugural celebrations. The event has always been a blend of pageantry and party. The inauguration of George Washington took place at Federal Hall in New York City, where an excited crowd chanted "Long live George Washington!" After reciting the oath of office, Washington added "So help me, God," a plea repeated by every president since. While George and Barbara attended fourteen inaugural balls, James Madison held the very first in 1809. His successor, James Monroe, took his oath on the steps of the old Capitol because of a disagreement over whether to use the "fine red chairs" in the Senate chamber, or the "plain democratic ones" in the House. Outdoor ceremonies would later become tradition. In 1829, thousands mobbed Andrew Jackson's "people's" inauguration, overrunning and wrecking the White House. Only punch on the lawn would lure them outside. In 1845, First Lady Sarah Polk carried a fan decorated with faces of the first eleven presidents (a gift from her husband), and at the turn of the century, Teddy Roosevelt wore a ring containing hair cut from the head of the assassinated president Abraham Lincoln. As the automobile age dawned, Woodrow Wilson was the last president to leave the ceremony in a carriage. Fifty years later, President and Mrs. Carter were the first since Thomas Jefferson to walk from the Capitol to the White House. In 1933, a constitutional amendment moved Inauguration Day from March to January 20. This turned out to be bad timing for Ronald Reagan, who delayed the festivities of his second inaugural in 1985 because they fell on Super Bowl Sunday!

First Lady to appear. And the wait was well worth it.

George and Barbara put in an appearance at each of the balls and danced together. Barbara Bush, who usually laughed at her appearance and made no fuss about clothes, looked beautiful that night. Her gown was a stunning shade of blue that suited her perfectly. The couple looked glam-

President and Mrs. Bush at one of the fourteen inaugural balls held on January 20, 1989

orous as they danced for the crowds of people cheering for them. The theme for the night was "George to George." It had been two hundred years since George Washington was president. Now another George was in that elected office and his wife, Barbara, was First Lady of the United States of America. This was an especially thrilling time for the Bushes because they felt they had achieved it together.

During George's campaign for president, he said he wanted to become the "education president." Many teachers from across the United States were invited to the inauguration festivities so that they would be able to tell their students about the events.

Over the 200-year history of America's First Ladies, their public images and political roles have been very different. Most have served as hostess in the White House, and many have acted as the president's partner. Some stayed in the background, simply tending to their children and households. Others have led very public lives. A few have caused the American public to worry about the control they might have over the president. The personal and political lives of many First Ladies merge; those wives become known by only what their husbands accomplished.

Throughout history, Americans have expected the First Lady to be a political wife who supports her hus-

Former First Ladies Betty Ford (left) and Rosalynn Carter testified before a Senate committee.

First Lady Hillary Rodham Clinton (left) at the UN World Conference on Women in Beijing

band's views. Today, the First Lady's role has changed with the way women are treated in this country. First Ladies can have opinions and careers, and are expected to be informed and willing to help solve some of the country's problems by getting out and working for a cause. Filling the position of First Lady can be exhausting, fun, and very challenging.

As First Lady, Barbara Bush acted much as she had throughout her

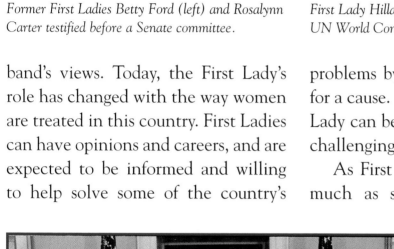

This Bush family photograph was taken a few days before George was inaugurated as president.

marriage. She was a supportive and helpful partner to her husband. Her share of the duties included campaigning, being his companion, and taking care of the household and family.

Barbara was a veteran political wife by the time she became First Lady, and she decided not to comment on issues that might cause trouble for George. She did not publicly take a side on such controversial issues as abortion rights for women or the Equal Rights Amendment. She did speak out on gun control, however, and that caused a problem. As First Lady, Barbara Bush knew she had a rare opportunity to promote the good of the country through her position.

As First Lady, Mrs. Bush continued her literacy work. She celebrated Black History month in Anacostia (a section of Washington, D.C.), and hosted a Reading is Fundamental (RIF) literacy group celebration on the South Lawn of the White House. She made many speeches and gave interviews about the literacy campaign. Barbara Bush felt very strongly that many of America's troubles including crime, pollution, unemployment, teen

pregnancy, AIDS, and homelessness could be improved if people were able to read and educate themselves about these problems. The RIF project was something that Barbara had worked for since 1966. With her help as First

Barbara hosted a RIF literacy group circus celebration on the White House lawn.

The Equal Rights Amendment

✫ ✫

The Equal Rights Amendment (ERA) was never added to the Constitution. First written in 1923, it stated that men and women shall have the same rights under the law. The amendment was approved by Congress in 1972. To become law, it would also need to be ratified (approved) by 38 states by the 1982 deadline. Only 35 states ratified the amendment before the deadline. Why would people vote against such a basic statement of equal treatment for men and women? Some feared that the amendment would force a negative change in the traditional roles of women. Many people believed that it would threaten family life and marriage. The industries that saved money by employing cheaper female labor lobbied against the ERA. Some women believed they would lose protections already in the law if the ERA passed. Others were concerned about women being drafted into military service. A few even predicted that men and women would have to share public bathrooms. One very vocal critic, Phyllis Schlafly, organized an emotional campaign against the ERA. She reinforced all of these fears and took advantage of the fact that few Americans understood how the ERA would change their daily lives. In fact, women in states that adopted similar amendments to their state constitutions won victories in areas of equal pay, more varied work and educational opportunities, and property ownership.

Lady, it continued to grow and to be very successful. Today, there are RIF projects in communities throughout the country.

Barbara also founded the Barbara Bush Foundation for Family Literacy in 1989. The foundation sponsors projects that earn money for family literacy programs and enabled her to continue her campaign to help people read and write. The year 1989 was called the Year of the Young Reader. As chairperson for this special year, Barbara worked on special projects. She visited schools all over the country and joined students in the Pledge

Barbara with students and staff at an adult literacy program in the Bronx borough of New York City

Barbara reading to day-care students at the Library of Congress celebration of the Year of the Young Reader

of Allegiance or read to Head Start children. Head Start is an organization that brings young, poor children to school before kindergarten to help them learn and get a "head start" on school. She hosted luncheons and sponsored many events for reading organizations and the foundation.

76

To the Flag

★ ★

We all know the 31-word Pledge of Allegiance so well, it's hard to imagine a time when children didn't recite it in classrooms or assemblies. Surprisingly, the Pledge has only been around a little more than a hundred years. It was written in 1892 by Francis Bellamy, a minister and educator. That year marked the 400th anniversary of Christopher Columbus's voyage to the New World, and President Benjamin Harrison declared that Americans should celebrate it appropriately. In that spirit, Bellamy developed a flag-raising ceremony, including the Pledge of Allegiance, for use in the public schools. At the same time, a school flag movement was gaining popularity. Until then, only military installations flew the flag every day, but many people supported the idea of a flag at every school. Today, most states require school buildings to fly the Stars and Stripes. The Pledge of Allegiance was officially recognized in 1942 when Congress passed a code describing rules for displaying and honoring the American flag. It dictates that people reciting the Pledge stand upright, remove headwear, and place the right hand over the heart. The words "under God" were added to the Pledge in 1954. Today, those words sometimes cause controversy among people with various views of religion.

First Lady Barbara Bush with her dog Millie

The book "written" by Barbara's dog Millie shows Barbara's sense of humor. Titled *Millie's Book: As Dictated to Barbara Bush*, it is a funny way to get children to read about what it is like to live in the White House. Millie tells about life in the president's house from the point of view of the first dog living among the humans upstairs. The book includes many

In 1989, Barbara threw out the first ball at a Texas Ranger-New York Yankee baseball game.

Millie's six puppies were born in the room that Nancy Reagan had used as a beauty parlor.

photographs of Millie's life as "First Dog" and her homes in Washington, D.C., Camp David, and Kennebunkport, Maine. The book earned almost $800,000 in royalties. The money was donated to the Barbara Bush Foundation for Family Literacy. If she hadn't given the money to this organization, she would have earned four times what the president makes in one year!

Barbara Bush has received much personal satisfaction from her work. She also has received honorary Ph.D. degrees from several colleges.

Not every visit or activity of the First Lady is serious and businesslike. In 1989, Barbara put on a Rangers warm-up jacket and threw out the first ball to start the baseball game against the New York Yankees! Barbara Bush also had fun with her dog, Millie. In fact, the room in the White House that was used by Nancy Reagan as a beauty parlor was turned into the birthing room for Millie when her six puppies were born. Barbara was there to help Millie.

In her first year in the White House, Barbara Bush was found to

This photograph of First Lady Barbara Bush holding an AIDS baby may have helped Americans to have less fear about touching and helping someone with AIDS.

have an illness called Graves' Disease. Although it is not life threatening, it does cause discomfort. Barbara chose not to pretend she was fine but instead let the country know about her illness and continued with her very busy schedule. She continued promoting literacy and fought hard to help people with AIDS as well. In one published picture, Barbara is holding an AIDS baby. Many people feel this picture helped Americans to better understand this tragic illness and have less fear about touching and helping someone with AIDS.

Barbara Bush seemed to be a happy woman who had been in training for the job of First Lady for most of her adult life. She took her job very seriously and still found time to be with her family and be an important part of their lives. She had a sense of humor about herself and her position and tried not to let things that were printed in the newspaper about her bother her. She knew people had jobs to do and reporting about her just happened to be part of their job.

The American public already knew and respected this First Lady from her

Barbara playing tennis in Kennebunkport during the summer of 1989

many years of serving alongside George Bush. The mother of five who had eleven grandchildren when she became First Lady was already well liked by most Americans.

By 1990, many young women felt that Barbara Bush's very traditional view of a First Lady's role was too old-fashioned. Barbara had been invited by the administration of Wellesley College to be the commencement speaker. When some of the students found out that she had been invited, they became quite angry saying that she did not represent the women of today. The students felt that Barbara Bush had never achieved anything on her own. They even started a petition against her appearance, which was signed by 150 students.

Whether or not Barbara Bush was hurt by these actions is not known, She did, however, smooth over the situation and win the applause of all who heard her speech. She told the students that she understood and respected their right to make a choice that had been different from hers. She even brought a friend to the graduation—Raisa Gorbachev, wife of the president of the Soviet Union. Both women spoke to the graduates. Mrs. Gorbachev, a university professor, and Mrs. Bush, a college drop-out, spoke of their work as First Ladies.

Perhaps the best line of Barbara

*First Ladies Barbara
Bush and Raisa
Gorbachev at
Wellesley College's
1990 commencement*

*The Bushes invited
Mother Theresa
(center) to the White
House in 1991.*

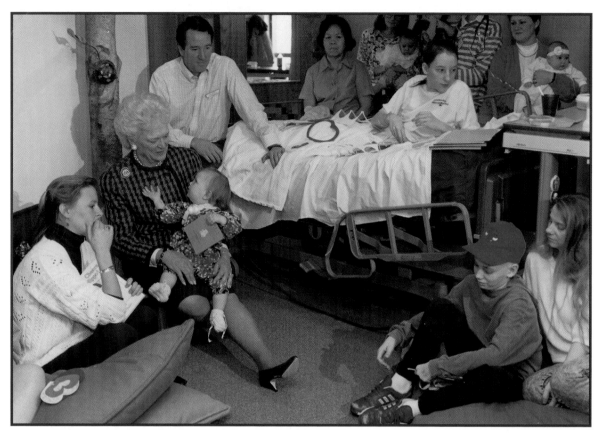

First Lady Barbara Bush visited this pediatric center in Lebanon, New Hampshire, during George's 1992 presidential primary campaign.

Bush's speech was the ending. She said to the graduates and their families, "somewhere out in this audience may even be someone who will one day follow in my footsteps and preside over the White House as the president's spouse." She paused, smiled, and added, "I wish him well." The audience laughed and cheered.

By 1992, Barbara looked forward to leaving the White House. She wanted to have time to garden, play with her grandchildren, and enjoy some quiet time with her husband. She did however, campaign as always for George in the 1992 presidential campaign. She believed him to be the best candidate, although he did not win the election.

Barbara Bush may have been one of the last First Ladies to have dropped

Millie enjoying a run while Barbara bicycles in Kennebunkport

Barbara and George campaigning in Houston

out of college to marry, raise a large family, and remain a silent partner to her husband. She was happy with her style and did not regret her choices. She was interviewed many times about her role as First Lady, and it is clear that she felt her methods were best for her and her husband.

George and Barbara leaving the White House on January 20, 1993

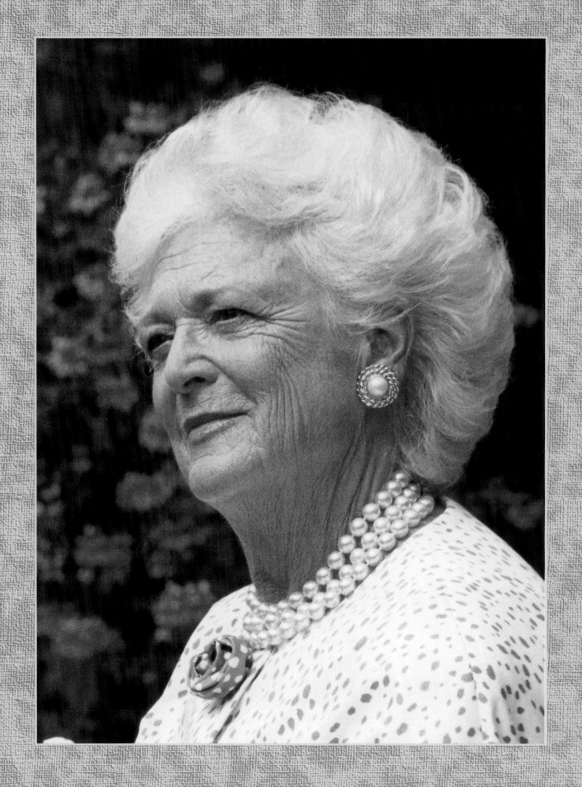

CHAPTER FIVE

After the White House

✫ ✫ ✫ ✫ ✫ ✫ ✫ ✫ ✫ ✫ ✫ ✫ ✫ ✫ ✫ ✫

Imagine having the opportunity to spend an evening talking with a First Lady! Students at George Washington University in Washington, D.C., had the chance to hear Barbara Bush and ask her questions as part of a special class on First Ladies. This class, held in 1994, was called the President's Spouse. The purpose of the class was to examine the role or job of the First Lady and to look at how each one had an impact or influence on the quality of her husband's presidency.

During the interview, Mrs. Bush was asked if she considered herself an author since she kept a diary and had written books and her memoirs. She replied that

✫ ✫ ✫ ✫ ✫ ✫ ✫ ✫ ✫ ✫ ✫ ✫ ✫ ✫ ✫ ✫

85

she never thought of herself as a writer and just felt those were things she had done as part of her literacy campaign. She also mentioned that she had once had her own radio show as First Lady called *Mrs. Bush's Story Time for Children*. During the program, she read stories that children could listen to at home. She also made and served meals to children at a homeless shelter in Washington, D.C., called Martha's Table.

The class professor, Dr. Carl Sferrazza Anthony, asked Mrs. Bush what she would have chosen to do with her life if she hadn't married George Bush.

As First Lady, Barbara Bush read stories to children on her radio show, "Mrs. Bush's Story Time for Children."

Mrs. Bush working at the Washington, D.C., homeless shelter called "Martha's Table"

She laughed and said that she had never really had a chance to think about what she would like to be when she grew up. She reminded the audience that she met George at age sixteen and was married at nineteen. Most teens at that age do not know what they want to become and she was not really any different. She became George's wife, which turned out to be a career in itself.

When the professor asked Barbara how she thought she did as a First Lady, she answered: "I always thought that one should do the best one can and that should be good enough. I did my own thing as First Lady and I think I did it well."

When the former First Lady was asked how she became an expert on literacy, she explained that she did not think she was an expert but just a cheerleader. She meant that being able to stand up and draw attention to the problem was what she felt she did well. She said that because the American people like the symbol of the First Lady, it is easier for her to help

Can You Read This?

⭐ ⭐ ⭐ ⭐ ⭐ ⭐ ⭐ ⭐ ⭐ ⭐ ⭐ ⭐ ⭐ ⭐ ⭐ ⭐ ⭐ ⭐ ⭐ ⭐

Remember a time when you couldn't read? Imagine what it would be like if you never learned how. Obviously, books and websites, newspapers and magazines would be beyond your reach. Think of all the little things that you would miss: street signs, instructions, maps, letters, menus, e-mail. Nor would you be able to write. How would you get through the day? Studies have shown that more than 20 percent of adults over the age of sixteen don't read well enough to earn a living wage. Four percent don't read at all. On the other end of the scale, only about 3 percent of Americans perform at the highest level of literacy competency. Common wisdom tells us that the best way to break the cycle of illiteracy is through family education, because if adults can read then their children are more likely to learn. In 1990, President Bush and the nation's governors set the goal for American adults to be literate by the year 2000. In 1991, Congress passed the National Literacy Act. In 1997, the federal government provided $469 million for adult education and family literacy. But there is still a long way to go. Sadly, fewer than 10 percent of all adults who need help learning to read are getting it.

people. After she chose literacy as her project, she found out that 90 million Americans don't read and write well enough to get or keep a job.

Many people think the First Lady can help them with their problems. Barbara Bush received a lot of mail from Americans including some from people with Graves' disease. Even people who have springer spaniels like Millie wrote to her. She still gets more letters than she can answer and has a staff to help her.

After leaving the White House, Barbara managed to live without so much attention from the public—and she loved the privacy. She believed that the press and television reporters were very fair to her, but she enjoyed her time with her many grandchildren

Barbara in her Kennebunkport garden

been a treat, and their life together is never boring.

Mrs. Bush still traveled and worked for her projects including her many literacy programs. Everywhere she went, children asked how Millie was doing! Mrs. Bush was also interested in world population control. In countries with very large populations, living standards are low because there isn't enough food to go around, nor are there enough jobs or educational opportunities.

Barbara Bush urged the people at her George Washington University

and her gardens. Barbara did say that leaving the White House was sad because the Bushes had spent twelve years in Washington, D.C., first as the Second Family and then as the First Family. Also, two of their children and several grandchildren lived in Washington. Happily though, one of their children and some grandchildren are in Texas, where the Bushes settled.

Barbara and George live in Houston in a new house they built after leaving the White House. Barbara said that living with George Bush has

Even after leaving the White House, Barbara maintained her interest in literacy.

89

Barbara playing golf after her White House years

interview to get involved in government. She told the audience that if they didn't like what is going on in their country, they must do something to change it. Getting involved in local government is the way to bring about big changes.

When asked what she thought her greatest accomplishments were, Mrs. Bush smiled and thought for a mo-

ment. Then she replied, "One of my greatest accomplishments is my five healthy children who give back to their communities and are family minded." The Bush family remained very close and spent time together whenever their different schedules allowed them to be in the same place.

Barbara Bush spends most of her summers in Kennebunkport, Maine, where she entertains family and friends, plays golf, and swims every day. She especially enjoys spending time with her children and grandchildren, who visit during the summers. To Barbara Bush's fourteen grandchildren, she is just a very busy but extremely loving grandmother who happens to have spent many years living and working in Washington, D.C. Barbara spent the summer of 1996 recovering from hip-replacement surgery.

When she returns to Texas early each fall, Barbara Bush takes up a busy speaking schedule, spending four to five days a week traveling. She speaks mainly about her literacy projects and also hosts a yearly fund-raiser called "A Celebration of Reading." The

and attention. Barbara Bush is still one of the most well-liked First Ladies. People like her for her honesty and her real concern about children and literacy.

Barbara's life after the White House years still included some political events and even some campaigning. In 1994, she did a few political events for her sons' campaigns for governor. Though George W. Bush was elected governor of Texas, Jeb Bush lost his campaign for governor of Florida. In 1998, George W. and Jeb ran again. George and Barbara again

Barbara Bush hosts an annual fund-raiser called "A Celebration of Reading."

money raised is used for the Barbara Bush Foundation for Family Literacy.

Wherever she travels, people are always excited to see her and meet her. She is a very friendly and warm woman who knows that people are excited to meet a former First Lady. She tries not to disappoint them even when so many people want her time

George and Barbara campaigning with George W. and his wife Laura in Houston

George, Barbara, and Millie are shown at their home in Houston in 1994.

The Bushes in Yuma just after George parachuted from an airplane in 1997

made campaign appearances in both Texas and Florida on behalf of their sons. This time, Jeb won his campaign and was elected governor of Florida. George W. Bush's landslide reelection as governor of Texas led to talk of his running for president in 2000.

As one of the nation's former First Ladies, Barbara Bush has been a popular speaker, with a full schedule of en-

gagements and national tours. Even so, she has found time for the new George Bush Presidential Library built on the Texas A & M campus in College Station, Texas. It contains all the important papers and documents from George Bush's days as president. Some of the gifts the Bushes received and their special honors are also kept there. The library also contains a sec-

Presidents on Exhibit

✦ ✦ ✦ ✦ ✦ ✦ ✦ ✦ ✦ ✦ ✦ ✦ ✦ ✦ ✦ ✦ ✦ ✦ ✦ ✦

For many of our twentieth-century presidents, there is a library and museum somewhere in the United States. These institutions keep important presidential papers and records for scholars to use. Some even serve as presidential burial places. In addition to documents and books dealing with the serious business of the presidency, you'll also find interesting exhibits about each president's life and times. Personal belongings, photographs, and family memorabilia are arranged to tell each president's story. Things such as Herbert Hoover's fishing tackle, George Bush's baseball glove, and the collar and toys of Franklin Roosevelt's dog give visitors a glimpse into their personal lives. Visiting a presidential library and museum is a fun way to experience some American history from the presidential point of view. Perhaps there is a presidential library or museum near you:

The Franklin D. Roosevelt Library	Hyde Park, New York
The Truman Library	Independence, Missouri
The Lyndon Baines Johnson Library	University of Texas, Austin campus
The Eisenhower Center and the Dwight D. Eisenhower Library	Abilene, Kansas
The Herbert Hoover Library	West Branch, Iowa
The John Fitzgerald Kennedy Library	Boston, Massachusetts
The Gerald R. Ford Museum	Grand Rapids, Michigan
The Jimmy Carter Presidential Library	Atlanta, Georgia
The Richard M. Nixon Library	Yorba Linda, California
The Ronald Reagan Presidential Library	Simi Valley, California
The George Bush Presidential Library	Texas A & M University, College Station

The Persian Gulf War: Fast Facts

WHAT: Operations Desert Shield and Desert Storm, mounted after Iraq invaded Kuwait

WHEN: August 2, 1990–April 6, 1991

WHO: A United States-led multinational coalition of forces faced the Iraqi army under President Saddam Hussein.

WHERE: During operation Desert Shield, American troops were deployed in Saudi Arabia to protect that country from Iraqi invasion and force Iraqi troops from Kuwait. The United States and its allies mounted Desert Storm, a military offensive that included a bombing campaign against targets in Iraq and Kuwait. A ground war soon followed, and the Allies liberated the capital at Kuwait City. The Iraqi army then set Kuwaiti oil fields on fire, leaving 500 wells burning out of control.

WHY: Iraqi president Saddam Hussein invaded Kuwait in a dispute over oil production and debt repayment. President Bush, the United Nations, and others believed that Hussein intended to invade Saudi Arabia next.

OUTCOME: A cease-fire was signed on April 6. Desert Shield claimed 108 American lives. More than 530,000 American troops served in Desert Storm; 266 died.

Current and former presidents and First Ladies at the dedication of the George Bush Presidential Library were, from left, Lady Bird Johnson, Jimmy and Rosalynn Carter, the Bushes, Bill and Hillary Clinton, Gerald and Betty Ford, and Nancy Reagan.

Barbara wore a camouflage jacket when she and George visited American troops stationed in the Persian Gulf. That camouflage jacket is now on exhibit at the George Bush Presidential Library.

tion dedicated to Barbara Bush. This exhibit highlights her contributions to literacy in America and her importance as a First Lady of the United States of America. Also included in the exhibit is the camouflage jacket Barbara wore when she traveled with George to visit American troops stationed in the Persian Gulf during Desert Storm.

The Presidents and Their First Ladies

President	Birth–Death	First Lady	Birth–Death
YEARS IN OFFICE			
1789–1797			
George Washington	1732–1799	Martha Dandridge Custis Washington	1731–1802
1797–1801			
John Adams	1735–1826	Abigail Smith Adams	1744–1818
1801–1809			
Thomas Jefferson†	1743–1826		
1809–1817			
James Madison	1751–1836	Dolley Payne Todd Madison	1768–1849
1817–1825			
James Monroe	1758–1831	Elizabeth Kortright Monroe	1768–1830
1825–1829			
John Quincy Adams	1767–1848	Louisa Catherine Johnson Adams	1775–1852
1829–1837			
Andrew Jackson†	1767–1845		
1837–1841			
Martin Van Buren†	1782–1862		
1841			
William Henry Harrison‡	1773–1841		
1841–1845			
John Tyler	1790–1862	Letitia Christian Tyler (1841–1842)	1790–1842
		Julia Gardiner Tyler (1844–1845)	1820–1889
1845–1849			
James K. Polk	1795–1849	Sarah Childress Polk	1803–1891
1849–1850			
Zachary Taylor	1784–1850	Margaret Mackall Smith Taylor	1788–1852
1850–1853			
Millard Fillmore	1800–1874	Abigail Powers Fillmore	1798–1853
1853–1857			
Franklin Pierce	1804–1869	Jane Means Appleton Pierce	1806–1863
1857–1861			
James Buchanan*	1791–1868		
1861–1865			
Abraham Lincoln	1809–1865	Mary Todd Lincoln	1818–1882
1865–1869			
Andrew Johnson	1808–1875	Eliza McCardle Johnson	1810–1876
1869–1877			
Ulysses S. Grant	1822–1885	Julia Dent Grant	1826–1902
1877–1881			
Rutherford B. Hayes	1822–1893	Lucy Ware Webb Hayes	1831–1889
1881			
James A. Garfield	1831–1881	Lucretia Rudolph Garfield	1832–1918
1881–1885			
Chester A. Arthur†	1829–1886		

† wife died before he took office   ‡ wife too ill to accompany him to Washington   * never married

1885–1889			
Grover Cleveland	1837–1908	Frances Folsom Cleveland	1864–1947

1889–1893			
Benjamin Harrison	1833–1901	Caroline Lavinia Scott Harrison	1832–1892

1893–1897			
Grover Cleveland	1837–1908	Frances Folsom Cleveland	1864–1947

1897–1901			
William McKinley	1843–1901	Ida Saxton McKinley	1847–1907

1901–1909			
Theodore Roosevelt	1858–1919	Edith Kermit Carow Roosevelt	1861–1948

1909–1913			
William Howard Taft	1857–1930	Helen Herron Taft	1861–1943

1913–1921			
Woodrow Wilson	1856–1924	Ellen Louise Axson Wilson (1913–1914)	1860–1914
		Edith Bolling Galt Wilson (1915–1921)	1872–1961

1921–1923			
Warren G. Harding	1865–1923	Florence Kling Harding	1860–1924

1923–1929			
Calvin Coolidge	1872–1933	Grace Anna Goodhue Coolidge	1879–1957

1929–1933			
Herbert Hoover	1874–1964	Lou Henry Hoover	1874–1944

1933–1945			
Franklin D. Roosevelt	1882–1945	Anna Eleanor Roosevelt	1884–1962

1945–1953			
Harry S. Truman	1884–1972	Bess Wallace Truman	1885–1982

1953–1961			
Dwight D. Eisenhower	1890–1969	Mamie Geneva Doud Eisenhower	1896–1979

1961–1963			
John F. Kennedy	1917–1963	Jacqueline Bouvier Kennedy	1929–1994

1963–1969			
Lyndon B. Johnson	1908–1973	Claudia Taylor (Lady Bird) Johnson	1912–

1969–1974			
Richard Nixon	1913–1994	Patricia Ryan Nixon	1912–1993

1974–1977			
Gerald Ford	1913–	Elizabeth Bloomer Ford	1918–

1977–1981			
James Carter	1924–	Rosalynn Smith Carter	1927–

1981–1989			
Ronald Reagan	1911–	Nancy Davis Reagan	1923–

1989–1993			
George Bush	1924–	Barbara Pierce Bush	1925–

1993–			
William Jefferson Clinton	1946–	Hillary Rodham Clinton	1947–

Barbara Pierce Bush
Timeline

1925	★	Barbara Pierce is born
1927	★	Charles Lindbergh becomes the first person to fly solo nonstop across the Atlantic Ocean
		Babe Ruth hits 60 home runs
1928	★	Herbert Hoover is elected president
1929	★	Stock market crashes and the Great Depression begins
1932	★	Franklin D. Roosevelt is elected president
		Amelia Earhart becomes the first woman to fly solo across the Atlantic Ocean
1933	★	President Roosevelt begins the New Deal to end the Great Depression
1935	★	Congress passes the Social Security Act
1936	★	Franklin D. Roosevelt is reelected president
1939	★	World War II begins
1940	★	Franklin D. Roosevelt is reelected president
1941	★	Japan bombs Pearl Harbor and the United States enters World War II
		Barbara Pierce meets George Bush
1942	★	George Bush joins the U.S. Navy
		Barbara Pierce and George Bush become engaged
		Japanese forces capture the Philippines
1943	★	Food rationing begins in the United States
1944	★	Franklin D. Roosevelt is reelected president
1945	★	Barbara Pierce marries George Bush
		Franklin D. Roosevelt dies
		Harry S. Truman becomes president
		Germany and Japan surrender, ending World War II

1946	★	George Walker Bush is born
1947	★	Jackie Robinson becomes the first African American to play major-league baseball
1948	★	George Bush graduates from Yale University Harry S. Truman is reelected president
1949	★	United Nations Headquarters is dedicated in New York City Pauline Robinson Bush is born
1950	★	United States enters Korean War
1952	★	Dwight D. Eisenhower is elected president
1953	★	Korean War ends John Ellis "Jeb" Bush is born Pauline Robinson "Robin" Bush dies
1954	★	Supreme Court declares segregated schools to be unconstitutional
1955	★	Neil Mallon Bush is born
1956	★	Marvin Pierce Bush is born Dwight D. Eisenhower is reelected president
1959	★	Dorothy Walker "Doro" Bush is born
1960	★	John F. Kennedy is elected president
1961	★	Berlin Wall separates East and West Berlin First Americans fly in space Peace Corps is established United States sends aid and troops to South Vietnam Roger Maris hits 61 home runs
1962	★	Cuban missile crisis forces the USSR to dismantle missiles in Cuba
1963	★	March on Washington is held for civil rights President Kennedy is assassinated Lyndon B. Johnson becomes president
1964	★	Lyndon B. Johnson is elected president Civil Rights Act of 1964 is passed

1965	★	Malcolm X is assassinated
		Riots break out in the Watts neighborhood of Los Angeles
		Protests begin over the war in Vietnam
1966	★	Congress passes the Medicare Act
		George Bush is elected to the U.S. House of Representatives from Houston, Texas
1968	★	Martin Luther King Jr. and Robert F. Kennedy are assassinated
		Richard M. Nixon is elected president
1969	★	President Nixon withdraws 110,000 soldiers from Vietnam
		U.S. astronauts land on the moon
1971	★	George Bush is appointed U.S. ambassador to the United Nations
1972	★	Last U.S. ground troops are withdrawn from Vietnam
		President Nixon visits the People's Republic of China
		Richard Nixon is reelected president
1973	★	President Nixon appoints George Bush chairperson of the Republican National Committee
1974	★	Richard M. Nixon resigns from office because of the Watergate scandal
		Gerald Ford becomes president
		President Ford grants Nixon a pardon
		President Ford appoints George Bush chief of the U.S. Liaison Office in the People's Republic of China
1975	★	South Vietnam falls to the Communists
		George Bush becomes head of the Central Intelligence Agency (CIA)
1976	★	Jimmy Carter is elected president
		United States celebrates its bicentennial
1978	★	People's Republic of China and the United States begin full diplomatic ties
1979	★	Iranians seize U.S. Embassy in Tehran and hold American hostages

1980	★	Ronald Reagan is elected president George Bush is elected vice president
1981	★	Iranians release the U.S. hostages Sandra Day O'Connor becomes the first woman appointed to the Supreme Court
1983	★	Sally Ride becomes the first American woman astronaut in space
1984	★	Ronald Reagan is reelected president
1986	★	Space shuttle *Challenger* explodes, killing all on board
1987	★	United States and Soviet Union sign nuclear missile reduction treaty
1988	★	George Bush is elected president
1989	★	Berlin Wall comes down
1990	★	Iraq invades Kuwait
1991	★	United States leads allies in the Persian Gulf War Iraq is pushed from Kuwait Soviet Union disintegrates
1992	★	Bill Clinton is elected president
1993	★	North American Free Trade Agreement is passed
1994	★	Baseball strike cancels the World Series George Walker Bush is elected governor of Texas
1995	★	U.S. terrorists bomb the federal building in Oklahoma City, killing 168 people Federal government shuts down because Congress and the president cannot agree on funding
1996	★	Bill Clinton is reelected president
1998	★	Sammy Sosa hits 66 home runs and Mark McGwire hits 70 George Walker Bush is reelected governor of Texas Jeb Bush is elected governor of Florida U.S. House of Representatives impeaches President Clinton

Fast Facts about
Barbara Pierce Bush

Born: June 8,1925, in Rye, New York

Parents: Marvin Pierce and Pauline Robinson Pierce

Education: Milton School and Rye Country Day School (both in New York); Ashley Hall (Charleston, South Carolina); Smith College (Northampton, Massachusetts)

Careers: Wrote a column for a Houston newspaper on life in Washington, D.C.

Marriage: To George Herbert Walker Bush on January 6, 1945

Children: George Walker Bush, Pauline Robinson "Robin" Bush (1949–1953), John Ellis "Jeb" Bush, Neil Mallon Bush, Marvin Pierce Bush, Dorothy Walker "Doro" Bush

Places She Lived: Rye, New York (1925–1941); Charleston, South Carolina (1941–1943); Northampton, Massachusetts (1943–1944); New Haven, Connecticut (1945–1948); Odessa, Texas (1948); California (1948–1950); Midland, Texas (1950–1959); Houston, Texas (1959–1966, 1977–1981, 1993–present); Washington, D.C. (1966–1971, 1973–1974, 1975–1977, 1981–1993); New York City (1971–1973); People's Republic of China (1974–1975); summers in Kennebunkport, Maine

Major Achievements:

⋆ Visited all fifty states and sixty-five other countries when her husband was vice president and hosted 1,192 events at the vice president's home.

⋆ Wrote the book *C. Fred's Story* from her dog's point of view and gave its earnings to two literacy programs.

⋆ Worked on literacy programs, especially Reading is Fundamental (RIF).

⋆ Founded the Barbara Bush Foundation for Family Literacy (1989) and served as chairperson for the Year of the Young Reader (1989).

⋆ Wrote *Millie's Book: As Dictated to Barbara Bush*, a book for children about life in the White House from her dog Millie's point of view, and gave its earnings to the Barbara Bush Foundation for Family Literacy.

⋆ Had her own radio show called *Mrs. Bush's Story Time for Children*.

⋆ Continued to promote literacy after leaving the White House.

Fast Facts about
George Bush's Presidency

Term of Office: Elected in 1988; served as the forty-first president of the United States from 1989 to 1993.

Vice President: Dan Quayle (1989–1993).

Major Policy Decisions and Legislation:

* Ordered U.S. troops into Panama, overthrowing the government of dictator Manuel Noriega (November 1989).
* Signed the Americans with Disabilities Act (July 1990).
* Ordered U.S. troops to Saudi Arabia as part of Operation Desert Shield after Iraq invaded Kuwait (August 1990).
* Signed a bill to reduce budget deficits by $500 billion over five years (November 1990).
* Ordered a cease-fire in the Persian Gulf War after Kuwait was liberated and Iraqi troops retreated (February 1991).
* Ordered U.S. troops, as part of a UN force, into Somalia (December 1992).

Major Events:

* *Exxon Valdez* strikes a reef in Alaska and causes the largest oil spill in U.S. history (March 1989).
* The Berlin Wall falls (1989) and East Germany and West Germany are reunited (1990).
* Bush appoints General Colin Powell as chairman of the Joint Chiefs of Staff, the first African American to hold that position (August 1989).
* Chinese troops crush student demonstrations in Tiananmen Square, killing about 700.
* Communist rule ends in the Soviet Union (1990).
* President Bush appoints two associate justices to the U.S. Supreme Court: David Souter (1990) and Clarence Thomas (1991).
* President Bush examines damage from rioters in South-Central Los Angeles (April 1992), caused after four white police officers were acquitted in the beating of African-American Rodney King.

Where to Visit

The Capitol Building
Constitution Avenue
Washington, D.C. 20510
(202) 225-3121

George Bush Presidential Library
    and Museum
1000 George Bush Drive West
College Station, Texas 77845
(409) 260-9552

Museum of American History of the
    Smithsonian Institution
"First Ladies: Political and Public Image"
14th St. and Constitution Ave. NW
Washington, D.C.
(202) 357-2008

National Archives
Constitution Avenue
Washington, D.C. 20408
(202) 501-5000

The National First Ladies Library
The Saxton McKinley House
331 South Market Avenue
Canton, Ohio 44702

White House
1600 Pennsylvania Avenue
Washington, D.C. 20500
Visitor's Office: (202) 456-7041

White House Historical Association
740 Jackson Place NW
Washington, D.C. 20503
(202) 737-8292

Online Sites of Interest

The First Ladies of the United States of America
http://www2.whitehouse.gov/WH/gimpse/firstladies/html/firstladies.html
A portrait and biographical sketch of each First Lady plus links to other White House sites

George Bush Presidential Library and Museum
http://csdl.tamu.edu/bushlib/bushlibrary.html
Located on the campus of Texas A&M University, it is part of a system of presidential libraries administered by the National Archives and Records Administration. Includes descriptions and pictures of the educational and entertaining contents of the museum and the research facilities of the library.

Internet Public Library, Presidents of the United States (IPL POTUS)
http://www.ipl.org/ref/POTUS/ghwbush.html
An excellent site with much information on George Bush, including personal information and facts about his presidency; many links to other sites including biographies and other Internet resources

The National First Ladies Library
http://www.firstladies.org
The first virtual library devoted to the lives and legacies of America's First Ladies; includes a bibliography of material by and about the First Ladies; also includes a virtual tour, with pictures, of the restored Saxton McKinley House in Canton, Ohio, which houses the library

The White House
http://www.whitehouse.gov/WH/Welcome.html
Information about the current president and vice president; White House history and tours; biographies of past presidents and their families; a virtual tour of the historic building, current events, and much more

The White House for Kids
http://www.whitehouse.gov/WH/kids/html/kidshome.html
Socks the cat is your guide to this site, which includes information about White House kids, past and present; famous "First Pets," past and present; historic moments of the presidency; several issues of a newsletter called "Inside the White House," and more.

For Further Reading

Blue, Rose and Corinne J. Naden. *Barbara Bush, First Lady*. Springfield, N.J.: Enslow Publishers, Inc., 1991.

Bush, C. Fred. *C. Fred's Story*. New York: Doubleday, 1984.

Bush, Millie. *Millie's Book: As Dictated to Barbara Bush*. New York: William Morrow & Company, 1990.

Gay, Kathlyn. *Persian Gulf War*. Voices from the Past series. New York: Twenty-First Century Books, 1996.

Gormley, Beatrice. *First Ladies*. New York: Scholastic, Inc., 1997.

Gould, Lewis L. (ed.). *American First Ladies: Their Lives and Their Legacy*. New York: Garland Publishing, 1996.

Heiss, Arleen McGarth. *Barbara Bush*. New York: Chelsea House Publishers, 1992.

Jacobson, Doranne. *Presidents and First Ladies of the United States*. New York: Smithmark Publishers, Inc., 1995.

Kent, Zachary. *George Bush: Forty-first President of the United States*. Encyclopedia of Presidents series. Chicago: Childrens Press, 1989.

Klapthor, Margaret Brown. *The First Ladies*. 8th edition. Washington, D.C.: White House Historical Association, 1995.

Mayo, Edith P. (ed.). *The Smithsonian Book of the First Ladies: Their Lives, Times, and Issues*. New York: Henry Holt, 1996.

McGowen, Tom. *World War II*. New York: Franklin Watts, 1993.

Sandak, Cass R. *The Bushes*. New York: Crestwood House, 1991.

Spies, Karen Bornemann. *Barbara Bush, Helping America Read*. New York: Dillon Press, 1991.

Stein, R. Conrad. *The Great Depression*. Cornerstones of Freedom series. Chicago: Childrens Press, 1993.

Index

Page numbers in **boldface type** indicate illustrations

Photo Identifications

Cover: Official White House portrait of Barbara Pierce Bush by Herbert E. Abrams
Page 8: Barbara Pierce at about age three
Page 30: Congressman George Bush and family
Page 50: An undated full-length photograph of Barbara Bush
Page 68: Official White House portraits of President George Bush and First Lady Barbara Bush by Herbert E. Abrams
Page 84: A 1991 photograph of First Lady Barbara Bush

Photo Credits©

White House Historical Association— Cover, 12, 68 (both pictures), 99 (bottom), 101 (top)
George Bush Presidential Library— 11, 14 (right), 21, 24 (bottom), 25, 27 (left), 28 (left), 30, 34 (both pictures), 35, 36 (both pictures), 38 (both pictures), 39 (top), 41 (left), 45 (bottom), 48 (top), 55 (bottom), 56, 57 (top), 59, 60, 62 (bottom), 64 (top), 65, 74, 77, 78 (top), 79, 81 (top), 83 (top and bottom right), 84, 86 (top), 89 (bottom), 90, 91 (left), 95 (bottom), 98 (both pictures), 99 (top and middle)
Julie Ianello— 13, 27 (right)
UPI/Corbis-Bettmann— 14 (left), 42 (top), 54 (top and bottom), 58 (top), 70 (top), 72, 80
Stock Montage, Inc.— 16, 45 (top)
Gamma-Liaison— 58 (bottom), 67, 89 (top), 95 (top); Lori Borgman, 18; Brad Markel, 24 (top), 61 (left), 70 (bottom), 73 (bottom), 86 (bottom); White House, 39 (bottom), 78 (bottom); Diana Walker, 55 (top), 64 (bottom); Steven Falk, 63; J. Barr, 66 (right); Dirck Halstead, 66 (left), 81 (bottom), 83 (bottom left); Jim Bourg, 82, 87; Cynthia Johnson, 92 (left)
Marilyn Gerrish— 19 (both pictures)
Rye Country Day School, Rye, New York— 20 (top)
Courtesy Ashley Hall— 20 (bottom)
AP/Wide World Photos— 22, 41 (right), 42 (bottom), 44, 46, 50, 54 (middle), 57 (bottom), 61 (top and bottom right), 62 (top), 76 (both pictures), 101 (bottom)
Yale University Library— 28 (right), 29
Corbis-Bettmann— 47
Archive Photos— 48 (bottom), 73 (top right); Reuters/Bruce Young, 73 (top left); Reuters/Michael Boddy, 91 (right); Reuters/Mike Nelson, 92 (right)
Reuters/Corbis-Bettmann— 52, 53
Reproduced by permission of the Richard Nixon Library, Yorba Linda, California— 100

About the Author

Judith Greenberg has more than 29 years of experience in education and has taught in both public and private schools in Washington, D.C.; Montgomery County, Maryland; Prince Georges County, Maryland; and the state of New Jersey. Her teaching career also includes master teaching and directing 21 grants on various subjects. She is the author and co-author of 37 library books for children and teens. For more than 25 years, Ms. Greenberg has worked with families seeking a better education for their learning-different or brain-injured children. In this capacity, she is the Founder and Director of SchoolFinders, an educational consulting firm in Potomac, Maryland, and Washington, D.C.

Judith Greenberg has written 25,000 test questions (something she hopes never to do again) and curriculum guides and kits. She also provides seminars for parents of "at-risk" students who wish to learn better ways of helping their children through the school process.

As an author, Judith Greenberg has received many national awards, including the coveted *Notable Children's Book* for 1996 for *A Pioneer Woman's Memoirs*, part of the Franklin Watts In Their Own Words series. Currently completing her doctorate in education, Ms. Greenberg is also the education consultant for the Environmental Protection Agency at its headquarters in Washington, D.C.

An avid swimmer and reader of mysteries and historical novels, Ms. Greenberg spends most of her free time with her nearly-grown son and daughter and shares her home with a yellow Labrador retriever and a brown and white American Staffordshire terrier. Judith Greenberg hopes you enjoy this book and adds that she loves to get e-mail from readers at: Schoolfind@aol.com.